Seva
CANADA

SAVING EYESIGHT

Adventures of Seva Around the World

Linda Pruessen

FIREFLY BOOKS

A Firefly Book

Published by Firefly Books Ltd. 2015
Copyright © 2015 Firefly Books Ltd.
Copyright © 2015 Seva Canada Society

FIRST PRINTING

Library and Archives Canada Cataloguing in Publication
Pruessen, Linda, author
  Saving eyesight : adventures of Seva around the world /
  Linda Pruessen.
Includes index.
ISBN 978-1-77085-615-8 (paperback). — ISBN 978-1-77085-616-5 (bound)
  1. Seva Canada Society—Juvenile literature. 2. Ophthalmology—Developing countries—Juvenile literature. 3. Blindness—Developing countries—Prevention—Juvenile literature. 4. Blindness—Developing countries—Treatment—Juvenile literature. 5. Eye—Diseases—Developing countries—Treatment—Juvenile literature. 6. Eye—Diseases—Developing countries—Prevention—Juvenile literature. I. Title.

RE48.P78 2015   j362.1977009172'4   C2015-903112-5

Publisher Cataloging-in-Publication Data (U.S.)
Pruessen, Linda.
   Saving eyesight : adventures of Seva around the world / Linda Pruessen.
[64] pages : color photographs ; cm.
Includes index.
Summary: "Saving Eyesight chronicles the efforts of Seva, an international development agency. Its mission is to restore sight and prevent blindness in the developing world. Young readers will learn about how the eye works and how eye problems are corrected. They will be touched by the true stories of those who have discovered sight after living in blindness" — Provided by publisher.
ISBN-13: 978-1-77085-616-5
ISBN-13: 978-1-77085-615-8 (pbk.)
1. Blindness—Juvenile literature. 2. Ophthalmology—Juvenile literature.
3. Eye—Wounds and injuries—Juvenile literature. 4. Seva Canda—Juvenile literature.
I. Title.
617.71 dc23   RE52.P784 2015

Published in the United States by
Firefly Books (U.S.) Inc.
P.O. Box 1338, Ellicott Station
Buffalo, New York 14205

Published in Canada by
Firefly Books Ltd.
50 Staples Avenue, Unit 1
Richmond Hill, Ontario L4B 0A7

Cover and interior design: LINDdesign

Printed in Canada

The publisher gratefully acknowledges the financial support for our publishing program by the Government of Canada through the Canada Book Fund as administered by the Department of Canadian Heritage.

CONTENTS

INTRODUCTION

Look around. What do you see? Maybe there are other people nearby, or maybe you're looking out the window at a big yellow sun in a bright blue sky. Can you pick out all the colors of the rainbow? Do you see how the light changes as the leaves of a tree blow in the breeze, or clouds pass over the sun?

For many people, the way we interact with the world is dependent upon sight. What we see when we look outside helps us figure out how to dress. We keep our eyes open when we walk down the sidewalk on the way to school so we don't bump into things. We read words on pages, screens and chalkboards to gain knowledge. Street signs help us figure out how to get where we're going.

It's frightening to imagine what life would be like if we couldn't see. But for many people, that scary thought is a reality. Right now, 285 million people around the world are visually impaired, and 39 million of those people are blind. Nearly 90 percent of blind people live in developing countries, where their lack of vision leaves them struggling for life's most basic needs, and keeps them trapped in poverty.

That sounds like pretty bad news—and it is—but there's also some good news: 80 percent of visual impairment can be treated, prevented or cured. Surgery can cure blindness. Glasses can correct visual impairment. Medicine can prevent blindness and treat eye disease. If everyone had access to good medical care and treatment, 31 million people who are struggling with blindness today would be able to see. And when more people are able to lead healthy, productive lives, entire communities have a chance at a better future.

In the pages that follow, you'll learn how organizations like Seva* are working hard to help the world's poorest people regain their sight, and, in the process, changing lives for the better. You'll learn how your eyes work (hint: they're pretty incredible) and about what can go wrong. And you'll learn how you can help.

Seva is a Sanskrit word meaning work performed without thought of repayment. In ancient India, Seva was believed to help one's spiritual growth and also contribute to the improvement of a community.

Seva Canada

Since 1982, Seva has been working to restore sight and prevent blindness in some of the world's poorest areas. They partner with local organizations to create eye care programs that are sensitive to the needs of the community and can lead to long-term change. They are committed to reaching those most in need: women, children and those living in extreme poverty and isolation. Seva's work has helped over 3.5 million people in areas like Nepal, Tibet, India, Malawi, Burundi, Cambodia, Guatemala and Egypt.

CHAPTER 1

THE AMAZING EYE

Eyes are often called the "windows to the world." And that makes sense. Just think of all of the things your eyes do. They let you see and respond to everything around you: your family, your friends, your teachers, a hockey or baseball game, a movie or a play. They show you yellow and red and purple. They make it easier for you to complete homework and do chores. They let you know when someone is smiling at you, or when a friend is sad.

One of the most amazing things about eyes, though, is that they do all of this without much help from you. You don't actually have to think about seeing; you just see. But how is this possible? How do your eyes work?

ANATOMY OF THE EYE

Your eyes are incredible pieces of equipment. Think about them like a very special camera: They take pictures of the world around you and send those pictures directly to your brain. Then your brain works out what your eyes are seeing. This process continues from the moment you wake up until the time you go to sleep. That's a lot of pictures!

Cornea

This is the see-through skin that covers the front of the eye. The cornea focuses light as it comes into the eye, to help you see.

Iris

The iris is the colored part of your eye, and the part that controls the amount of light that enters. The most common eye color in the world is brown.

Pupil

The pupil is the black opening in the center of the colored iris that lets light into your eye. It gets very small in bright light, and bigger in dull light.

Lens

If you couldn't control the light coming into your eyes, you wouldn't be able to see anything. Your eyes need to focus on what you're looking at, and the lens helps them do that. When you're looking at something close (like a computer screen or a book), your lens changes shape and gets smaller and rounder. When you're looking at something farther away, the lens becomes flatter.

Sclera

This is the tough skin that covers the outside of the eyeball (except for the cornea). You may have heard it called the "white" of the eye.

Retina

The retina is where light signals are turned into nerve impulses that the brain can understand. The retina is home to two types of receptors: the "rods" are able to see black and white, and the "cones" are able to see color.

Optic disk

The optic disk is the circular area in the back of the inside of the eye where the optic nerve connects to the retina.

Optic nerve

The nerve impulses from the retina travel along the optic nerve to your brain. It's sort of like the cable that carries all the pictures from the Internet to your computer so you can see them.

Vitreous cavity

This is the area behind the lens and in front of the retina. It's filled with a gel-like liquid called the vitreous humor, which helps keep the eye in shape.

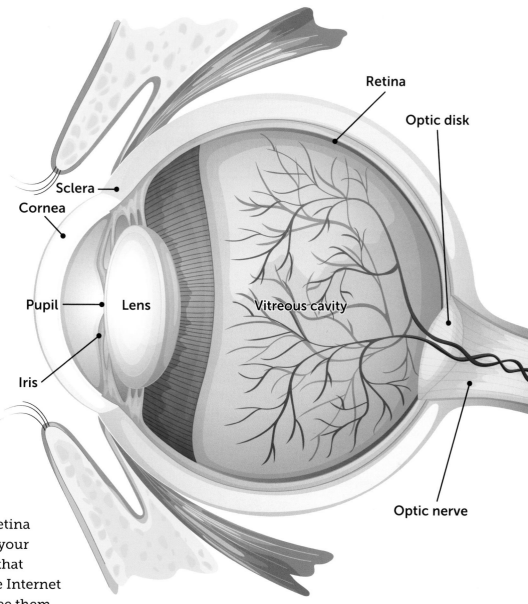

Retina

Optic disk

Sclera

Cornea

Pupil

Lens

Iris

Vitreous cavity

Optic nerve

Security Team: Lids, Lashes and Brows

Your eyes are protected by a small but dedicated army. Your eyelids shut very fast if they sense something heading toward your eyes. Your eyelashes trap dust and trigger a "close" response in your eyelids when necessary. And your eyebrows trap dust and keep salty sweat from dripping into your eyes. Ouch!

EYE FACTS AND FIGURES

Now that you know how your eyes work, let's learn more about these amazing instruments.

All Caucasian babies are born with blue eyes.

On the Job

Seeing is such a big part of your life that almost half of your brain is involved in the process. And your muscles are in on the action, too. The muscles that control your eyes are the most active in your entire body.

Baby Blues?

This may be hard to believe if you have a brand new brother or sister hanging around, but newborns don't cry. Sure, they make crying sounds—a lot of them! — but actual tears don't start to flow until babies are between four and 13 weeks old.

Another strange fact? All Caucasian babies are born with blue eyes. This is because they are not born with the amount of melanin (the pigment that gives color to your skin, hair and eyes) they will eventually have. That develops over time, and eye color changes as it does, based on those genes we just discussed.

Blue, Green or Brown?

Ever wondered why some people have blue eyes while others have brown? Or why you're the only person in your immediate family with your eye color? It's all about your genes. Each person has two genes that determine eye color. If you've got two identical genes, you'll have eyes of that color. If you've got two different genes, the dominant gene will take the prize. Brown genes are always dominant, while blue genes are recessive. This means if you've got one brown gene and one blue gene, you're going to have brown eyes.

Things get tricky when you look back into your family's gene pool. Your mom and dad, for example, may have brown eyes, but if they've both got a recessive blue gene lurking in their system, those genes have a 25 percent chance of getting passed down to you. If they do, you'll have blue eyes.

Eye Transplants? Not So Fast!

Your eyes are one of the body's many organs. Organ donations and transplants are discussed all the time, but eyeballs aren't part of the discussion. The optic nerve that connects that eye to the brain is too delicate and sensitive for doctors to reconstruct. If you've heard stories about someone receiving an "eye transplant," what they're likely talking about is the cornea. Right now, it's the only part of the eye that can be transplanted.

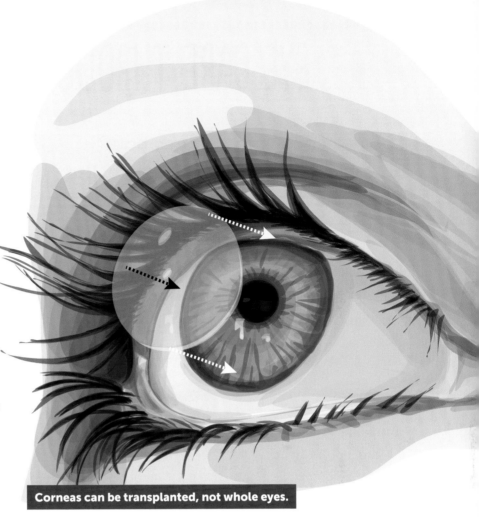

Corneas can be transplanted, not whole eyes.

In the Blink of an Eye

The average blink lasts for about a tenth of a second, and you blink about 25 times every minute that you're awake. Why do you blink? Sometimes it's because something has gotten into your eye, and the blink helps clear it away. Mostly, though, blinks happen because the tear glands in the corners of your eyes are always making tears. The opening and closing of your eyelids wipes those tears away and keeps your eyes moist and clean. Blinking is a reflex. You don't have to think about it—it just happens!

Today, people know more about how eyes work than ever before. But people have been studying the eye for centuries.

Eye cups or eye baths are popular in England for the application of liquid eye medicines or for cleaning. The patient applies the cup to the eye with their head bent forward. Then they lean back and open their eye, allowing the liquid to wash over the eyeball.

German mathematician Johannes Kepler discovers the **path that light takes through the eye**, and is the first to recognize that images are "seen" upside down, and then reversed by the lens onto the retina.

Dozens of Islamic scholars write treatises on **ophthalmology**, trying to understand the functions of the various parts of the eye.

| c. 170 AD | c. 900–1300 | 1286 | 1508 | 1578 | 1604 |

The first pair of **eyeglasses** is reportedly made in Pisa, Italy.

Greek physician, surgeon and philosopher Galen of Pergamon writes about **eye treatments**. He names many parts of the eye, and even performs a form of cataract surgery that is similar to what is used today.

Did Leonardo da Vinci Invent the Contact Lens?

No, but he may have played a part in its development. In 1508, the famous Italian architect, mathematician and inventor drew diagrams suggesting that the way the eye sees could be altered if the cornea came into direct contact with water, or if a person could wear a water-filled glass over the eye. Although contact lenses were not invented for another 350 years, da Vinci's basic idea of altering the eye's focus point remained the principal behind the use of lenses.

Soft or Hard?

A little over a hundred years ago, the only type of contact lenses available were "hard." Although they were initially made of glass, changes in technology over the years means that they are now made out of rigid but flexible plastic. They are less comfortable than soft contact lenses, but are better for certain types of vision problems. "Soft" lenses, invented in 1961, are preferred by most people because of their comfort.

Many soldiers return from the Napoleonic wars with an infectious eye disease known as **trachoma**. In part as a response to the epidemic, the Royal London Ophthalmic Hospital is established—the first hospital in the world devoted entirely to the treatment of eye disease.

The **vision test card** is invented.

Swedish ophthalmologist and optician Allvar Gullstrand receives the **Nobel Prize** in Physiology or Medicine for his work in applying the principles of physical mathematics to the study of optical images and the refraction of light in the eye.

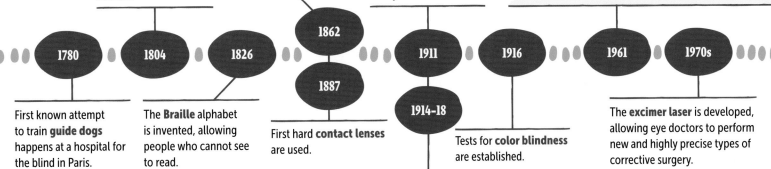

1780 | **1804** | **1826** | **1862** | **1887** | **1911** | **1914-18** | **1916** | **1961** | **1970s**

First known attempt to train **guide dogs** happens at a hospital for the blind in Paris.

The **Braille** alphabet is invented, allowing people who cannot see to read.

First hard **contact lenses** are used.

Tests for **color blindness** are established.

The **excimer laser** is developed, allowing eye doctors to perform new and highly precise types of corrective surgery.

Canine Companions

During World War I, many soldiers lost their sight due to the use of poison gas. German doctor Gerhard Stalling worked at a veterans' hospital. One day, he was visiting with a blind patient when he was called away suddenly. He left his German shepherd to keep the soldier company. When he returned, he got the feeling that the dog was trying to help the man. By 1916, Stalling had opened the world's first school for guide dogs. Although Stalling's school closed less than ten years later, others followed, throughout Europe and, eventually, in North America.

A VISIT TO THE EYE DOCTOR

Eye doctors, as you've seen, have been around for a while. But what goes on in that office? What is the doctor looking for when she shines that little light in your eye, and what do all of those machines really do?

An Opto-What?

First things first. Just who are you seeing when you visit the eye doctor? Depending on the choice your family has made, you may be seeing an optometrist or an ophthalmologist. Optometrists have earned a Doctor of Optometry degree. They can examine eyes for vision and health problems, prescribe eyeglasses and contact lenses and prescribe medications to treat certain eye problems. Ophthalmologists are medical doctors who specialize in eye and vision care. They can do everything optometrists can do, but can also perform eye surgery. And let's not forget the opticians. They use the prescriptions written by your eye doctors to create your eyewear.

Testing, Testing

If you are visiting an eye doctor for the first time, you'll likely fill out a questionnaire about your medical history. Once that's done, it's on to assessing how your eyes are working—separately and together. To do this, eye doctors perform a number of tests. Here are a few of the most common:

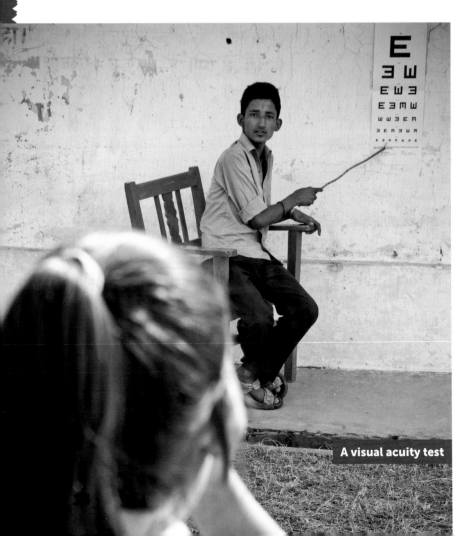

A visual acuity test

A cover test

A refractive test

Visual acuity: You know those eye charts, the ones with the big E at the top? Those are used to test visual acuity—or the sharpness of your vision. The one on the wall is used to measure how you see distant objects, and a small handheld one is used to measure your "near" sight.

Cover test: Don't be surprised if your doctor asks you to focus on a small object across the room, and then covers one of your eyes while you're doing it (and then repeats the process for the other eye, and for an up-close object). By noticing how your eye moves to focus on the target, your doctor is watching how your eyes work together.

Refractive test: This test determines your eyeglass prescription. The doctor puts an instrument called a phoropter in front of your eyes and flips through a series of lenses, asking you which of the two allows you to see better. Based on your answers, the doctor will fine-tune the lens power until a final prescription is determined. A refraction test can assess hyperopia (farsightedness), myopia (nearsightedness), astigmatism and presbyopia.

Slit lamp exam: The slit lamp, also called a biomicroscope, provides a highly magnified view of the structures of your eye, allowing your doctor to detect any signs of infection or disease. A slit-lamp examination can reveal signs of cataracts, macular degeneration, corneal ulcers, diabetic retinopathy and more.

20/20 Vision

In the world of eye care, the phrase "20/20 vision" is used to describe normal vision. It means that the patient being tested can see the same line of letters on a vision chart at 20 feet as a normal person. The second number is the one to watch. A person with 20/40 vision, for example, can see at 10 feet what a normal person sees at 20 feet, which means her vision is worse than normal. (A person with 20/15 vision, however, has better vision than the average person).

Do You Need an Eye Exam?

The only way to know for sure is to see an eye doctor. But here are some hints that it might be time to make that appointment!

- You have trouble seeing things that are close to you (like a book), or things that are far away (like a chalkboard).

- You have trouble seeing at night.

- You get a headache if you've been staring at a computer or the television for too long.

- You have trouble playing sports that involve eye-hand coordination.

- You sometimes lose your place or skip lines when reading.

- You often rub your eyes, or squint.

- Your eyes feel too dry, or too watery

If you're experiencing any of these issues, talk to your parents.

WHEN THINGS GO WRONG

When your eyes are working properly—when all of those parts explored a few pages ago are in alignment—you'll see well. But if something's off, problems can arise. Here are some of the most common eye problems facing people around the world today.

Twenty million people around the world have cataracts.

Cataracts

You've learned about how light travels through the pupil and the lens to get to the retina, where light signals are turned into nerve impulses that travel to the brain. But what happens when light is unable to enter the eye? With cataracts, the lens gradually becomes cloudy, and that clouding blocks the light. Without treatment, the clouding can eventually lead to blindness. In fact, 20 million people around the world have cataracts, and they are the cause of 51 percent of global blindness.

The good news is that treatment of cataracts is easy, if you have the right tools. Once an ophthalmologist diagnosis cataracts, they can be treated with a surgery that removes the cloudy lens and replaces it with an artificial one. The surgery can be done in 15 minutes and costs only $50 in the developing world. In North America, the costs are considerably higher, but even so, you won't see too many people with cataracts, thanks mostly to the availability of eye care services. In less developed parts of the world—where many people are unaware that some eye problems can be treated, and where eye care facilities are hard to come by—diagnosis and treatment can be a challenge.

Glasses are a simple solution to refractive error.

Refractive Error

"Refractive error" is a fancy way of talking about what happens when the light from whatever you're looking at doesn't get properly focused on the retina. The two most common types of refractive error are nearsightedness and farsightedness. Some 124 million people around the world have visual impairment due to refractive error, and it's the main cause of vision problems in children. If you happen to have one of these conditions, you might suffer from headaches, difficulty reading or trouble seeing the chalkboard in your classroom.

You know what helps? Glasses. Sounds like a simple enough solution, and for many people it is. But what if you don't live in an area where good eye care can be easily accessed? What if you only have a few dollars a day to spend, and you have to choose between glasses or food?

Infection: Trachoma

In North America, eye infections aren't usually that serious, and can be treated with antibiotic eye drops. In other countries, though, the situation is different.

Trachoma is a bacterial infection of the eye and the leading cause of preventable blindness in the world. It causes the inner surface of the eyelids to become rough, and leads to scarring of the eye as the lids open and close. Trachoma can be spread from person to person, and also via flies. It's found in areas that feature poor hygiene practices, crowded households, a shortage of clean water and inadequate separation of bathrooms and bathing facilities. Trachoma is only one of many infectious eye diseases.

Trachoma can be treated with antibiotics—where available—but if the underlying conditions of the infection are not addressed, it is likely to reoccur, and likely to cause more permanent damage.

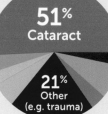

CHAPTER 2

WHO IS BLIND?

As you go about your daily life, you probably don't give too much thought to your eyes. You either wear glasses or you don't. You and your friends may think of glasses or contacts in the same way that you do braces—if you need them, you'll get them. End of story.

In other parts of the world, though, things aren't so straightforward. Blindness is a disease of poverty. The exact reasons why there are more blind and visually impaired people in the developing world aren't clear, as it could be a combination of many causes such as diet, daily life, genetics and exposure to Ultraviolet (UV) light.

 # POVERTY AND BLINDNESS

Do you know that of the nearly 285 million people in the world who are visually impaired, almost 90 percent live in developing countries? It's a vicious cycle—poverty and disease can lead to vision loss, and blindness and poor vision can keep people trapped in poverty.

The World Health Organization has stated that restoring someone's sight is one of the most cost-effective ways to reduce poverty.

The Missing Links

Why do so many people in low-income countries suffer from vision problems? Often, it's because they have difficulty accessing good eye care.

There may be very few—if any—eye doctors available. It's common in these countries for general practitioners (what we would call "family doctors") to take on the work of caring for their patients' eyes, but doctors may not be properly trained to do so, and may not be aware of the latest treatment options.

It's also likely that the men, women and children who need eye care would not be able to afford it, even it if were available. The doctor might be too far away, or the family might not be able to spend its income on glasses or medication when putting food on the table is a higher priority.

Finally, in some parts of the world, fear and uncertainty can play a role. If you'd never seen an eye exam machine, for example, do you think it might seem a bit scary?

Happy patients after their cataract surgery at a Seva eye camp in Banteay Meanchey, Cambodia.

Access to Eye Care

Access to eye care is a key factor when it comes to preventing vision impairment. But it's clear that people living in high-income countries have a much better chance of accessing care that is provided by knowledgeable health care workers. Those in the developing world may not realize that they have a problem and that it can be treated, and this is compounded by their lack of money or transportation to access help.

A Nepalese girl having her vision tested at a school screening.

This map shows where Seva works around the world. There are many other developing countries that are still in need of eye care.

WHEN CHILDREN CAN'T SEE

Imagine yourself as a young child—maybe five or six years old. Now imagine losing your sight. That's what happened to Tenzen Chudren, a six-year-old girl from Tibet. When cataracts made it impossible for Tenzen to see, her entire personality changed.

She lost all of her curiosity about the world around her and became scared and nervous. She didn't want to leave her house. She clung to her mother constantly. The change was difficult on the whole family. Tenzen's mother could no longer work or even care effectively for her other two children. She spent all of her time looking after Tenzen's needs.

Fewer Chances

More than 19 million children around the world suffer from blindness or impaired vision, like Tenzen. If you've ever squinted at the blackboard at the front of your classroom or struggled to read a textbook, you'll understand that children who have trouble seeing are often unable to succeed at school—if they can go at all. Not surprisingly, these kids have fewer opportunities to succeed in life.

Good News

The good news is that many of the causes of childhood blindness or visual impairment are treatable. With the help of Seva, Tenzen was able to have cataract surgery on both eyes. Shortly after, her mother reported that she was once again curious about everything around her, and ready to tackle new challenges.

Before cataract surgery, Tenzen is scared.

WOMEN AND BLINDNESS

Here's an astonishing fact: two-thirds of the people who are blind are women. Why? In many parts of the world, men control the income of the house. They may be the only ones making money, and may not allow the women to decide how to spend it.

It's also true that in some cultures, women are considered less "valuable." In these cultures, being born a girl means being less likely to get an education. Sometimes girls might get less food than their brothers, and oftentimes you are denied things that are given to sons. Imagine a family like this in which two children—one a boy and one a girl—need glasses, but only one pair can be afforded. Who do you think is more likely to receive them? You guessed it: the boy. In cases like this, girls who are blind or visually impaired don't get glasses, don't get medications they may need and don't have the opportunity to access healthcare services or treatments for their blindness.

After cataract surgery, Tenzen was once again curious about the world.

The Ripple Effect

It's bad enough that young girls with easily treatable eye conditions may not be receiving the help that they need, but what happens when those girls grow up? Young women with visual impairment may find themselves unable to marry, or to work to help support their families.

Mothers who can't see may have trouble taking care of their children. They may have difficulty in preparing food and keeping the home clean—both of which can create conditions in which eye problems can occur.

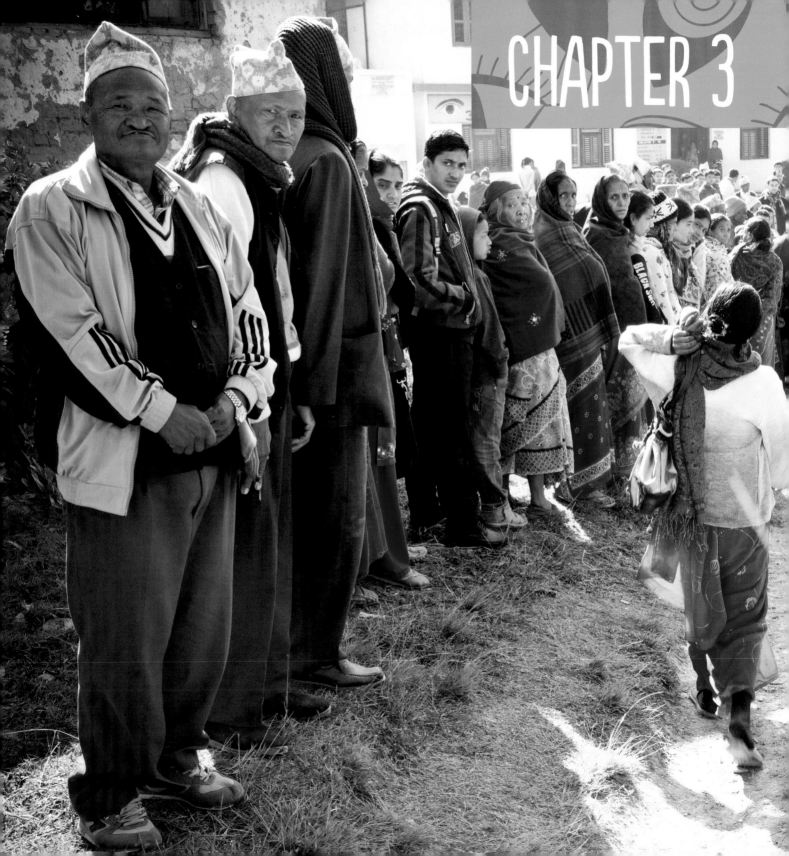

CHAPTER 3

A HELPING HAND

You've read about how, for many people, visual impairment is a treatable problem—if there is access to good medical care. But in numerous places around the world, there aren't nearly enough medical doctors to treat the population, and doctors who deal specifically with eye health may be even harder to come by. In some countries, there is only one (or even less) ophthalmologist per one million people! Imagine how difficult it would be to make an appointment with that doctor, or schedule time for a simple procedure. Now imagine how hard it would be for a family to pay for a cataract surgery.

Fortunately, there are organizations around the world that are working hard to help.

EYES ON THE WORLD

Seva has made providing access to good, affordable eye care its mission. This map shows the countries where Seva is active, teaming up with local partners to make sure that their positive work continues into the future.

Visual acuity test being performed in a Cambodian village.

A Guatemalan girl is happy with her new glasses.

Guatemala: Seva works with Visualiza Eye Care System to provide eye care programs and treatment.

A Malagasy key informant attending a screening camp.

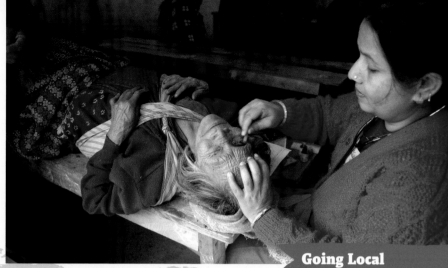

Nepal: Seva has worked with Seva Nepal to develop 25 eye care facilities providing care to over 5 million people.

Tibetan Areas of China: Seva supports Seva Tibet to fund two-thirds of all cataract surgeries in the region.

Cambodia: Seva supports eye care programs and training in the provinces of Banteay Meanchey, Siem Reap, Pursat, Kampot and Battambang.

India: Along with their partner, Aravind Eye Care System, Seva trains eye care providers from most of its partner countries.

Eastern Africa: Seva funds eye surgeries, glasses, the training of eye care professionals and childhood blindness programs in Tanzania, Malawi, Madagascar, Burundi and Ethiopia. In Africa, Seva works with the Kilimanjaro Centre for Community Ophthalmology (KCCO) based in Moshi, Tanzania, and Cape Town, South Africa, to support these eye care programs.

Some organizations that provide humanitarian and medical aid to poor areas of the world do so by supplying help from the outside. Sometimes people are sent in to help; other times, medication, food or other supplies are delivered to a particularly needy community. Seva prefers to train local experts to provide eye health services, to make glasses or to provide treatments. When this approach is taken, the community improves for the long-term, not just for as long as the aid organization is in town.

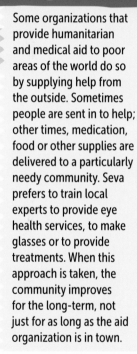

Thumbnail Sketch: India

India is a fascinating country—the world's seventh largest by area, and its second largest by population (China is first). Within its boundaries visitors can find numerous religions, cultures and languages. Cities such as Mumbai and Delhi are known for their hustle and bustle, while rural areas such as Assam and Darjeeling are famous the world over for the fine tea they produce. The Taj Mahal—perhaps India's most famous tourist attraction—is one of the wonders of the world.

Population: 1,224,614,327

India

It is estimated that over 31 million people in India have severe visual impairment due to cataracts. There are 8 million blind people in India with approximately 4 million who are blind due to cataracts. Back in the 1970s, a retired eye surgeon in India had an idea. He wanted to make cataract surgery as "ubiquitous [common] as McDonald's," and therefore affordable to even the country's poorest citizens. Dr. G. Venkataswami—known as "Dr. V."—met with Seva and, shortly after, a long-standing partnership to provide high quality eye care to all was born. Today, that clinic is known as Aravind Eye Care System. It's doing amazing things on the eye care front throughout the country, and in 2008, the organization won the Gates Award for Global Health, which honors extraordinary efforts to improve health in developing countries.

Patients lining up for eye care at Chitrakoot, a hospital mentored by Aravind.

A Model for Change

Aravind is now the busiest eye care organization in the world, serving more than 2.5 million men, women and children each year. Together, Seva and Aravind have developed a system in which fees are charged only to those who can afford them. Two-thirds of the people treated by Aravind have received their care for free. Thanks in part to Aravind's efforts, the estimated number of blind people in India fell from 8.9 million in 1990 to 6.7 million in 2002, a decline of 25 percent.

Aravind started as an 11-bed hospital in a rented house. Six beds were reserved for patients who could not pay and five for those who could afford a modest fee. Today, Aravind is a network of eye hospitals with close to 4,000 beds. In 2010, it provided more than 300,000 eye surgeries. In addition, the clinic now acts as a mentor to other eye care institutions.

Reaching Out

But all the hospitals and clinics in the world won't help if people don't know that help is available. Surprisingly, the vast majority of people blind from cataracts in rural India have no idea why they are blind, or that a surgery

A community eye health worker examining a young boy.

can restore their sight in a few minutes. The question, then, is how to reach these people.

Aravind holds eye camps—40 per week around the states of Tamil Nadu and Kerala. The camps visit villages every few months, offering eye exams, basic treatments and fast, cheap glasses. Patients requiring surgery are invited to come to the nearest of Aravind's hospitals; all transport and lodging, like the surgery, is free.

As helpful as this sounds, it wasn't enough. When Aravind studied the impact of its camps, it found that only 7 percent of people in a village who needed care were being treated, mainly because the camps weren't frequent enough. To provide a permanent presence in rural areas, Aravind established 36 storefront vision centers. They are staffed by rural women recruited and given two years' training by Aravind. They have cameras, so doctors at Aravind's hospitals can do examinations remotely. Within a year, about 30 percent of people needing help were getting it.

MANGOBINDA PAL

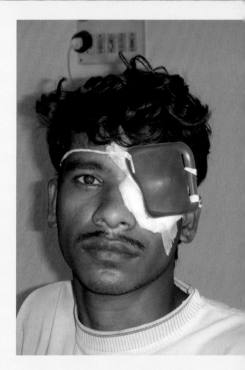

Mangobinda Pal lives in the village of Kakkhuy Do. His life has not been easy. He suffers from macular dystrophy, a type of corneal scarring that eventually leads to blindness. When he was 18, the corneal scarring became so severe that Mangobinda was completely blind. His condition and his inability to provide for his family caused them terrible distress.

Mangobinda's father-in-law made it his life's mission to find help for his son-in-law. They spent four years searching for a hospital that could do a corneal transplant, but corneal surgery was either not available or far too expensive. A family member recommended the Vivekananda Mission Ashram. Not only did they have the expertise, but they also provided the surgery for free.

Now that Mangobinda's sight has been restored, he wants to work to support himself and his family, and he wants to repay his father-in-law for the kindness he has shown him.

Nepal

On a bright, chilly day in the village of Thulobesi, a team of workers from the Lumbini Eye Institute had set up stations in the classrooms of the local school. Vision testing, refractive services and surgical areas all had their places. Curious villagers and anxious patients crowded around with anticipation.

In the pre-surgical room, where ophthalmic assistants prepared patients for cataract surgeries, Gyani, a poor woman in her early twenties, and her two-year-old daughter, Gothi, were both diagnosed with bilateral cataracts. Gyani had never seen her child before, and she was very nervous about the outcome of surgery. The doctors did their best to reassure her. While Gyani has the procedure, Gothi, cradled in her uncle's arms, cried for her mother.

Early the next morning, Gyani's bandages were removed and a huge smile lit up her face when she saw her daughter for the first time.

A Nepalese nurse checking a patient's eye pressure.

Bringing the Care to the Patients

One of the best and most important ways to treat eye conditions in a country like Nepal is through grassroots work—getting into the villages and towns where people live and bringing services to them. An organization like Seva, for example, can partner with local groups to ensure that the people who most need it are able to access care.

The Lumbini Eye Institute trains ophthalmologists and ophthalmic assistants, but it also supports nine eye care facilities, including three secondary hospitals and six Primary Eye Care Centres (PECC). A PECC is able to treat almost all eye health issues, including minor conditions, provision of eyeglasses and referral of more serious conditions to the hospital.

In 2013–14, working with local partners, Seva has:

- examined 471,000 patients;
- performed 46,000 cataract surgeries;
- screened 65,761 patients at eye camps;
- examined 155,000 children through school screening programs; and
- provided 2,900 pairs of glasses, free of charge.

A Dire Situation

Today, both Gyani and Gothi are able to see and live more enriched, productive lives. It's a success story, for certain, but others like it are still all too rare. Nepal is consistently listed among the world's poorest countries, so it's no surprise that good health care, including eye care, is hard to come by. More than 16 percent of the population suffers from one or more eye disease, with 3 percent either totally or partially blind. As in other countries, however, most of these cases of visual impairment are preventable and curable. And thanks to the work of organizations like the Lumbini Eye Institute, Nepal is making great strides in this area. In fact, it has become the model for eye care program development in the region.

Nepalese cataract patients at an eye camp patiently waiting for their bandages to be removed.

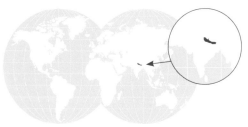

Thumbnail Sketch: Nepal

Think of Nepal and you probably think of mountains. This tiny country is located in the midst of the Himalayas mountain range and is home to eight of the world's 10 tallest mountains, including Mount Everest—the highest point on earth. Its largest city is Kathmandu.

Population: 26,494,504

SIGHT STORY
RAM BAHADUR

Many years ago, Ram Bahadur lost his left eye in an accident while breaking rocks to make concrete. It became infected, and though he went to traditional healers, he was too poor to seek help from eye specialists. Eventually the infection worsened and he lost the eye. Then a cataract robbed him of his vision in his right eye.

Ram's wife cared for him, leading him by the hand, guiding him to his food, taking him to the washroom and looking after all of his needs. Finally, she brought him to an eye camp near the town of Arghakhanchi, where Ram received cataract surgery. Afterward, he was carried to his friend's home to spend the night, waiting and hoping for a new life.

In the morning light, the husband and wife waited quietly to have his bandages removed. The moment the eye patch was taken off he was able to see her face! A few minutes later, he stood up and began walking around on his own, heading over to the eye chart. Ram was happy, but his wife was thrilled; no more leading her husband to the washroom!

35

Tibet

Norbu, 16, Metok, 14 and Tashi, 27, stood in the hospital hall, holding hands and trying to present themselves as well as they could. Their uncle, Chilu Dorjee, had brought them to the eye camp, a 50-mile (80-km) drive along dangerous and bumpy roads. All three siblings were blind.

Tashi blamed himself for not being a good father to his own children. "I am nothing but a burden," he said. "I have lost many things over the years, but most of all I have lost my dignity for being blind. Every morning I wake up feeling hopeless and worthless inside."

When his younger siblings also became blind, Tashi knew exactly what they were going through. Norbu and Metok had the normal hopes and dreams of children their age. With their blindness, Tashi knew, these dreams would never come true.

At the eye camp, all three were diagnosed with bilateral cataracts. They each underwent surgery on one eye the next day and on the second eye the day after that. With their eyesight restored, smiles soon returned to their faces.

Norbu, Tashi and Metok are happy.

Making a Difference

Norbu, Tashi and Metok are just three of many Tibetans who have been helped by eye care efforts in the Tibetan regions of China. This area, located in the western part of China, has one of the highest rates of blindness in the world, mainly due to untreated cataracts.

Tibet is enormous—1.5 million square miles (2.5 million km^2). Its extremely poor population is widely spread throughout the area, rather than gathered in a few main cities, and that fact, combined with a lack of public transportation, makes it difficult to provide help.

Seva began working in the region in 1995, and has partnered with local organizations such as the Tibetan Development Fund and the Public Health Bureau, to establish services to train doctors. Thanks to ongoing work like this, more than 50,000 Tibetans have had their sight restored.

Focusing on the Children

While childhood blindness is a concern in many countries, Tibet has been particularly hard hit. In the Tibet Autonomous Region (TAR) alone—located in the extreme west of the Tibetan regions of China—there are approximately 5,000 blind children. It's believed that 75 percent of them could have their sight restored, with access to proper care.

For a long time, however, that care simply wasn't available. None of the

Dr. Martin Spencer training Dr. Tzering.

Dr. Yangki-la helping a child.

Thumbnail Sketch: Tibet

For many who live in the West, Tibet remains one of the world's unexplored places. This large region of China is entirely surrounded by mountains, and its enormous lakes are the starting point for some of Asia's mightiest rivers. Its administrative and religious capital—Lhasa—dates back to the mid-seventh century.

Population: 6,000,000

local ophthalmologists were able to provide surgical care to children. Most of these families had no choice but to wait—sometimes for as long as a year—for foreign doctors to visit Lhasa, the TAR's largest city. That wait can worsen the chances of a successful treatment.

In 2008, all of that changed. With the help of Seva, the Menzikhang Hospital of Traditional Tibetan Medicine in Lhasa launched a Childhood Blindness and Low Vision program. The goals were to provide eye care to Tibetan children and to train local ophthalmologists to work on their own. The program also works hard to bring eye care to local communities by running school screening camps and training local healers and teachers to spot the signs of eye disease and refer kids for care.

SIGHT STORY
DATSO

Twelve-year-old Datso lives in Tibet with her family and new baby brother—a brother she has never seen. Before he was born, cataracts in both eyes caused her to go blind.

Datso's uncle heard about a Seva eye camp in their region and brought her to the hospital. "When other kids are playing outside of her home, she just cries and cries," he told the workers. "She can't stop asking us why she is different and why she has to be blind."

Although Datso was excited about the possibility of having

surgery, she was also worried that it might not work. "I am not capable of doing anything but sitting in my home with my grandparents all the time," she said. "Nobody is willing to play with me. I can't see now and I am afraid that I will never see again."

After successful cataract surgery on both eyes, Datso and her family were overjoyed. Datso herself was looking forward to "doing everything," but there was one thing, in particular, that had to come first. "I need to see my one-month-old brother at home!"

39

Cambodia

I t's never a good sign when children stop playing. But that's exactly what was happening with Samarith Romchong, a five-year-old Cambodian girl. She was gradually losing interest in playing with her siblings and friends. Her parents were worried; she was becoming more clumsy, knocking things over and falling down a lot. Her falls caused several injuries.

Romchong's parents are very poor, and they struggle to care for their five children with their tiny plot of land. They live in a small village with no road access. Desperate to help their youngest child, they sought help from traditional healers and went many times to different pagodas to give prayers and offerings that might help their child. They even sold their cow in their search for a cure.

One day, a relative who lives near the Banteay Meanchey Eye Unit visited the family. When they looked carefully at the girl's eyes, they noticed whitish pupils. The relative suggested that it seemed like a cataract. If so, she could be treated.

Soon after, the family made the 45-mile (75-km) journey to the eye care center, where Romchong underwent successful cataract surgery on both eyes. At her follow-up visit, her parents reported that she was back to being a happy little girl.

A Seva Cambodia field worker conducting visual acuity testing in a village pagoda.

The After-Effects of War

Romchong is one of 90,000 people in Cambodia blinded by cataracts; another 22,000 new cases are added each year.

Many of Cambodia's current troubles stem from its unsettled and violent past. From 1975 to 1979, the brutal dictator Pol Pot and his Khmer Rouge tore apart the country in an effort to create a new state. All businesses were closed, education and health care disappeared, and hospitals were emptied. After Pol Pot's regime fell, there was one ophthalmologist in the country—a foreign doctor. Thirty years later, Cambodia's population is still paying the price for the Khmer Rouge's reign of terror.

Building Up in Banteay Meanchey

Seva Cambodia facilities conduct outreach activities in remotes areas and refer patients to the closest eye units/clinics for further evaluation and sight restoration. Some of the facilities conduct vision screenings at primary schools and provide children with free eyeglasses. Seva Cambodia saw a dramatic increase in the utilization of eye care, particularly cataract surgical rates, in all of its districts following the hiring and training of four field workers. The costs of the field workers, eye surgery and transportation have been supplemented by Seva funding.

Five-year-old Romchong after surgery: A happy little girl.

Thumbnail Sketch: Cambodia

Located in Southeast Asia, Cambodia is known for its temples, its rice fields and a brutal civil war in which two million people perished. Angkor Archeological Park is a World Heritage Site, containing the remains of the different capitals of the Khmer Empire (from the 9th to the 15th century). The most famous of these, Angkor Wat, is the seventh wonder of the world (see previous spread).

Population: 15,205,539

SIGHT STORY
MONG KONG SEAV

Not all eye problems require surgery. Mong Kong Seav, a 14-month-old Cambodian girl, had a tearing, watery left eye that was causing her family a great deal of concern. When a Seva-sponsored village screening took place near her home, her grandmother, Lau Kha, took her to have her eye looked at while her parents were working in the fields.

Mong's bottom eyelid had not fully developed and was not thick enough to keep her tears in her eye. The field nurse advised her grandmother that Mong's eye should fix itself and she was given antibiotics to prevent infection.

Happy and relieved, Mong and Lau went home to tell the little girl's parents that her eye and vision were going to be okay.

Tanzania

T he magnitude of the blindness problem in Africa is overwhelming. Besides the many challenges of poverty, there are simply not enough eye doctors to go around. Only about one in ten people blinded by cataracts ever receives surgery. There is a desperate need for programs to train local people to provide eye care to their own communities.

The Kilimanjaro Centre for Community Ophthalmology (KCCO)

In 2001, Seva helped establish the KCCO, the only training institution for community ophthalmology in Africa dedicated to reducing blindness. It serves 7 eastern African countries with a population of close to 210 million, from Egypt to South Africa.

KCCO has helped many hospitals in Africa double or triple the number of people who have received sight-restoring surgery. Doctors and other eye care professionals come from countries across the continent to learn.

KCCO also has a network of community-based programs reaching out particularly to women, who are most at risk of blindness because they do not have access to care.

Children watching an eye screening in a village. The one child is doing his own visual acuity test.

A Little Help from Our Friends

Organizations like Seva can do a lot of good, thanks to donations from people who care about their mission, but sometimes, extra help comes in handy. Companies in the eye care business often step up to help with donations of eyeglasses, medications and other supplies. Alcon, which specializes in eye care products, has donated medical supplies, OGI Canada has donated eyeglass frames, and back in 1980, Steve Jobs donated an Apple II computer that spent 33 years in Nepal!

Madagascar

I t's hard to image, but more than 92 percent of Madagascar's population lives on less than $2 a day. Not surprisingly, they have little ability to travel to or access eye care services. With help from the Kilimanjaro Centre for Community Ophthalmology in nearby Tanzania, however, local programs are being set up.

Thumbnail Sketch: Madagascar
Madagascar is a special place. The world's fourth-largest island, the country is home to a huge variety of flora and fauna. In fact, 5 percent of all known animal and plant life exists in Madagascar only.

Population: 22,005,222

Screening Programs and Key Informants

In Madagascar, Seva supports the training of "key informants"—men and women in rural villages who go door to door to identify those in need of eye care and refer them for examination. Each key informant can be responsible for about 5,000 people, making the program an effective way to reach those who might otherwise not get the care they need.

SIGHT STORY HERY

E leven-year-old Hery Mamy Moreno Randriamboavonjy lives in the slums in Antananarivo, the capital of Madagascar, with his nine-year-old sister and his grandmother, Lucie. Hery's mother passed away when he was younger, leaving Lucie to raise the children. She struggles to provide for Hery and his sister.

For as long as he can remember, Hery has wanted to be a doctor. "Ever since he could talk Hery used to ask other children what was ailing them so he could fix them. He works really hard at school so he can become a doctor. He's second in his class," said Lucie proudly.

But last year, a schoolmate punched Hery in the left eye, resulting in a traumatic cataract that robbed him of his vision. After that, he would bump into furniture and had trouble seeing the board at school and reading his textbooks. He wasn't even allowed to play his favourite sport— soccer—with his friends.

Hery's sight was restored with a 15-minute cataract surgery paid for by Seva donors. "I'm happy to have the surgery so I can see again, I'm not scared at all," said Hery the day of his operation. The next day, when his eye patch was removed, Hery and his grandmother were ecstatic. "I'm going to continue to study hard and am confident I will become a doctor. And now I can play soccer with my friends!" exclaimed a smiling Hery.

Burundi

Like Cambodia, Burundi has been torn apart by civil war. After 12 years of fighting between the Tutsi and the Hutu, the country is now trying to piece itself back together. It is one of the world's poorest nations and relies on help from the rest of the world to fund health care, education and other programs.

Thumbnail Sketch: Burundi

Burundi sits just south of the Equator in central Africa. It's a landlocked country where most of the population works in agriculture, producing coffee, cotton, tea and sugar. It is home to an amazing number of bird species.

Population: 10,395,931

SIGHT STORY
DR. LEVI KANDEKE

This is a different story—not of someone who needs help, but of someone who is giving it. Dr. Levi Kandeke is Burundi's first ophthalmologist trained to perform surgery. When the 39-year-old met a fellow ophthalmologist from Cameroon who was working in a very senior position at the World Health Organization he told Levi that the best and most important years of his life were those spent providing eye care to the people of Cameroon. He inspired Levi to return home and use his training where it was needed most.

Levi returned to a country still recovering from civil war with a government that could not afford adequate health care for most of its citizens. While there were a number of trained ophthalmologists, none were trained to perform even the simplest of surgical procedures. Only the wealthy

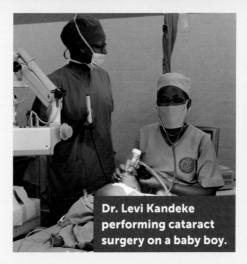

Dr. Levi Kandeke performing cataract surgery on a baby boy.

Dr. Kandeke (right) with pediatric cataract patients.

could access services in Tanzania or Rwanda.

Levi introduced big changes to Burundi's eye health program. He opened a private clinic in the capital Bujumbura to subsidize surgeries for those too poor to pay. With his own savings, he built Africa's first two vision centers—at either end of the country. With Seva's funding, he held Burundi's first two pediatric eye camps and restored sight to hundreds of children.

Malawi

Every year, approximately 150 children in Malawi are born with or develop cataracts. It is the leading cause of blindness in children in the country. And yet, when the Queen Elizabeth Central Hospital in Blantyre started to offer eye care services for children in 2008, only 81 kids received surgery. What about the others? Without help, they face a lifetime of blindness.

The Childhood Blindness Program

The Childhood Blindness Program in Malawi is dedicated to reducing childhood blindness through early identification of children with visual impairment and providing treatment and follow-up. One of the main challenges, however, is finding the children who need help. Children cannot speak for themselves, and their parents may be more concerned about the children's overall health than his or her eyesight.

Donations from Seva and its partners are helping by training health care workers and volunteers to seek out children with eye problems. Nearly 7,000 children have had their eyes examined, more than 200 have had corrective surgery and nearly 100 have received prescription glasses.

Thumbnail Sketch: Malawi
Located in southeast Africa, the landlocked country of Malawi is among the world's least developed. The population lives largely in rural areas, and the prime source of income for most residents is agriculture. The nation faces challenges when it comes to improving education and health care, and becoming financially independent. The government currently depends heavily on foreign aid programs.

Population: 16,407,000

A 2½ year old boy just after bilateral cataract surgery.

51

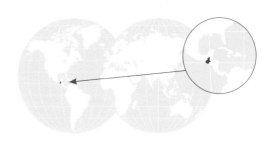

Guatemala

In the Petén, the northernmost area of Guatemala, a Visualiza Eye Care System program called Little Windows of Light helps more than 15,000 of the country's poorest children each year through eye screening and follow-up care. Elsewhere, Dr. Mariano Yee of Visualiza Eye Care System works hard to make sure the poor can access the help they need. The efforts are paying off. Visualiza does about 30 percent of all cataract surgeries in the country—with only 2 percent of the nation's opthalmologists.

Thumbnail Sketch: Guatemala
Guatemala is located in the middle of Central America, bordered by Mexico to the north and Honduras to the south. Water lies to the east and west. Once part of the huge Mayan empire, the country is now a vacation hot spot that offers visitors the chance to explore jungles, volcanoes and caves, experience white-water rafting and zip-lining and check out some amazing architecture.

Population: 15,806,675

SIGHT STORY
ESTEFANY

Estefany is 12 years old. She lives in a two-room wooden house with her three brothers, father and stepmother. Because of her eye conditions, she has been teased and called "ugly" by her schoolmates and even by members of her own family. Her parents once took her to a clinic, but they were unable to get assistance. Her father, who is a farmer, makes less than $8 a day. Her stepmother is a maid who makes even less.

Estefany was brought to Visualiza in December 2008

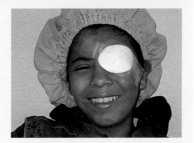

and diagnosed with both strabismus (squint) and ptosis (drooping eyelid). In February 2008, she had two surgeries, both successful. She does much better with her school work now, and her beautiful smile speaks volumes.

Locals watch a Mayan celebration in this small Guatemalan village.

Egypt

Unlike some of the other countries you've explored, Egypt could likely restore vision to many of its 800,000 blind people. There are a number of eye care professionals working in the country. Unfortunately, most of them are in Cairo and the other major cities. That leaves many of the people who need eye care—namely those living in rural areas and, especially, women—unable to get help, even when its free.

Eye Care Caravans

The Al Noor Magrabi Foundation is doing its best to help. It runs a charity hospital as well as outreach caravans and special programs designed to address the problem of blindness among women, girls and the very poor. In Egypt, outreach caravans and local vision centers are vital in reaching out to people who live in disadvantaged regions with little or no medical eye care services. Outreach teams travel throughout Egypt to do eye screenings, provide medicine and glasses. Those that need surgery are then referred to a hospital for further care.

Thumbnail Sketch: Egypt

Hear the word "Egypt" and you immediately imagine the time of King Tutankhamen and the pharaohs. You picture the Sphinx, the Nile and the amazing pyramids. But Egypt is also a modern country. Its capital city, Cairo, is the largest in the Middle East, and the Suez Canal, which connects the Red Sea with the Mediterranean, is one of the world's largest shipping routes.

Population: 81,121,077

SIGHT STORY
HOSNA ABD ELAZEEM

Hosna Abd Elazeem first noticed her vision deteriorating when she started having trouble sorting rice for cooking. It seemed like something was floating in front of her eye, obscuring her vision. Nothing seemed to fix it, so she eventually just tried to accept the issue.

Fortunately for Hosna, her village was visited by the outreach field team from Al Noor Magrabi Foundation.

When the outreach workers knocked on Hosna's door, she told them about her problem. There, she was examined by doctors, who diagnosed her with cataracts and diabetes. After controlling her diabetes, Hosna was able to undergo sight-restoring cataract surgery at the Al Noor Hospital.

Hosna was delighted with the results and grateful she'd been able to get treatment in time.

"I have no complaints about my sight now and can even see colors brighter than before," she said. She added that in the future she would encourage her relatives and neighbors both to check for diabetes and to seek medical advice whenever they have eye problems.

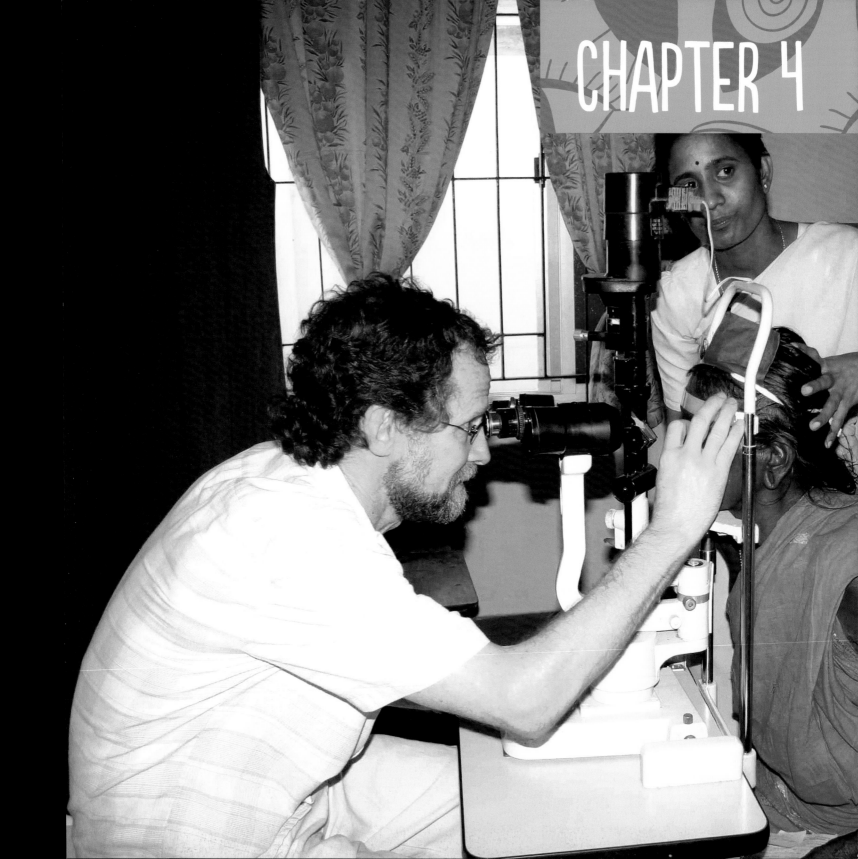

CHAPTER 4

GET INVOLVED

Throughout this book, you've learned a lot about how your eyes work, about how eyesight can fail, and about how people in certain parts of the world are more likely to suffer from vision problems—and how those problems can keep people trapped in a life of poverty. You've also learned how access to good eye care can make a difference. You've read stories about people whose lives have been changed dramatically for the better thanks to a simple, affordable surgery or medication. You know now that everyone should have access to eye care.

Making that happen depends on people just like you—people who are willing to pitch in and help. Luckily, there are lots of ways you can help.

Learn More

You've certainly learned a lot throughout this book, but there is always more to know! Go on the Internet and visit some websites to find out more about how important good eye care is, especially for those living in the world's poorest countries. Many of these websites also have suggestions about how you can help. You can also use your computer or your local or school library to learn more about how your eyes work.

Help Raise Money

Organizations that dedicate themselves to helping others—like Seva—are always in need of funds to keep their efforts going. There are many ways you can help by raising money to support their work.

On your next birthday, consider asking your friends and family to make a donation instead of giving you a gift. Do some research ahead of time to make sure you know how to get that donation into the right hands, and make sure to follow up with your guests to let them know where their money went and what it's being used for.

Ask your teacher or school principal if they are interested in holding a bake or book sale to help raise funds. Or, if you belong to a sports team or community group, see if you can help organize a performance to benefit the cause.

Sell Gifts

Many non-profit organizations produce gifts that they sell to help raise money. Seva, for example, sells cards, journals and calendars to supports their work in Asia, Guatemala and Africa. You can contact Seva to find out about selling those gifts in your community.

WORLD
SIGHT
DAY

World Sight Day takes place every year on the second Thursday of October. It's a day of awareness that focuses attention on the global issue of avoidable blindness and vision impairment. Visit the World Sight Day website ahead of time to see what events might be planned for your neighborhood. There are often walks, bike rides and rallies.

Your Money at Work

If you decide to fundraise, you should be prepared to answer questions about what the money you are raising is going to be used for. Here are a few examples from Seva:

$15 provides medicine to prevent blindness.

$25 provides prescription glasses for five people.

$50 provides eye screening in orphanages and schools.

$50 restores an adult's vision with a 15-minute cataract surgery including lens implant, follow-up care, medications and transportation.

$50 helps to train female eye care advocates.

$100 helps support an eye screening camp.

$100 helps to train a community field worker to find people with blindness and eye disease and help get them to the hospital for care.

$100 helps to train an ophthalmic nurse or assistant to provide eye care to a community. With this knowledge, they can diagnose and treat 90 percent of all eye conditions.

$150 cures a child's blindness with cataract surgery, including a specialized pediatric lens implant and follow-up care, including glasses, medications and transportation.

 # GLOSSARY

Astigmatism A vision condition that causes blurred vision due either to the irregular shape of the cornea, the clear front cover of the eye, or sometimes the curvature of the lens inside the eye.

Cataract An abnormal loss of clarity of the natural lens inside of the human eye. Typically develops later in life and can reduce vision due to the inability of light to enter the eye.

Cornea The clear dome of tissue at the front of the eye that is the first element of the focusing system; provides two-thirds of the eye's focusing power.

Cylinder The amount of lens power necessary to compensate for astigmatism.

Farsightedness A vision condition in which distant objects are usually seen clearly, but close ones do not come into proper focus.

Glaucoma A group of disorders leading to progressive damage to the optic nerve, and is characterized by loss of nerve tissue resulting in loss of vision.

Inflammation The eye's natural reaction to trauma, often accompanied by discomfort, redness and swelling.

Iris The colored portion of the eye behind the cornea.

Lens The part of the eye behind the iris that adjusts focus for different distances by changing shape.

Nearsightedness A vision condition in which you can see close objects clearly, but objects farther away are blurred.

Optic Nerve The bundle of 1 million nerves that transmits information from the retina (back of the eye) to the visual center of the brain.

Pupil The black opening in the center of the iris that allows light into the eye; its size increases under dim lighting.

Refraction The test used to determine the amount of nearsightedness, farsightedness and/or astigmatism.

Retina The light sensitive, back part of the eye containing the rods and cones that turns light waves into brain waves allowing us to see.

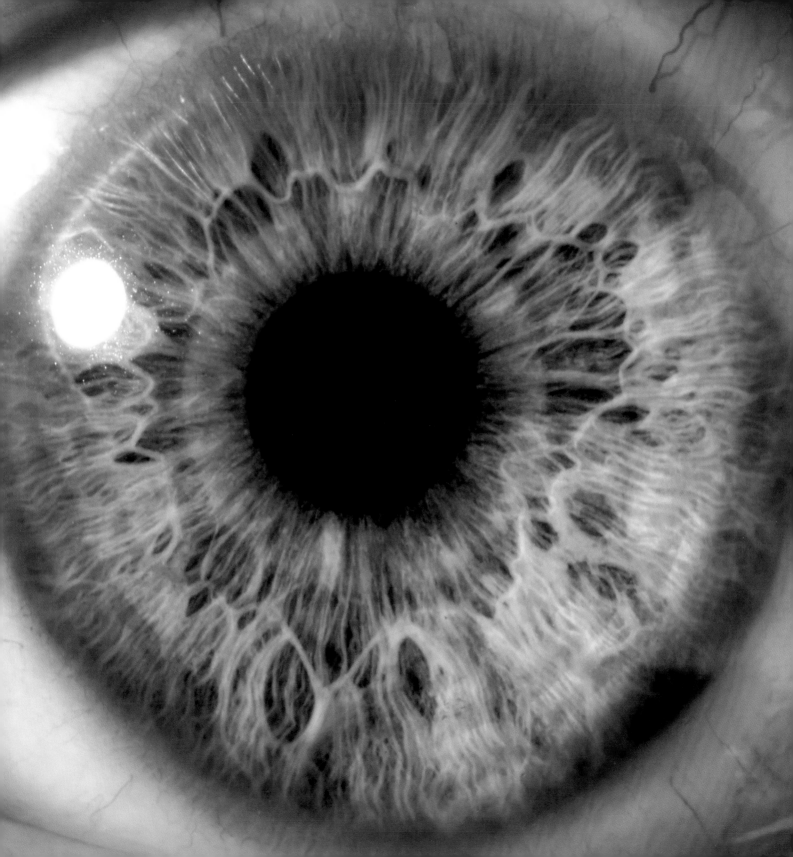

 # ABOUT SEVA

Seva Canada is an international development organization that restores sight and prevents blindness in the developing world. Since 1982, Seva donors have given the power of sight to over 3.5 million people in low-income countries.

Seva's vision is a world in which no one is needlessly blind or visually impaired.

It works with local partners to create sustainable eye care programs that achieve long-term change, are culturally sensitive and reach those most in need—women, children and people living in extreme poverty and isolation.

Seva believes that giving sight to a blind person is the most effective way to relieve suffering, reduce poverty and transform lives. To that end, it uses a public health approach to provide the best care for the most people; no one is turned away from services if they cannot pay. Seva helps its partners work toward self-sufficiency by training local people in clinical skills and program management, and assists programs in procuring their own equipment and supplies to lower the cost of care.

Seva works in 13 of the poorest places in the world: Nepal, Tibetan Areas of China, India, Malawi, Madagascar, Zambia, Burundi, Ethiopia, Tanzania, Guatemala, Cambodia, Rwanda and Egypt.

PHOTO CREDITS

 INDEX